IMAGES
of England

WOLVERHAMPTON
A CENTURY OF CHANGE

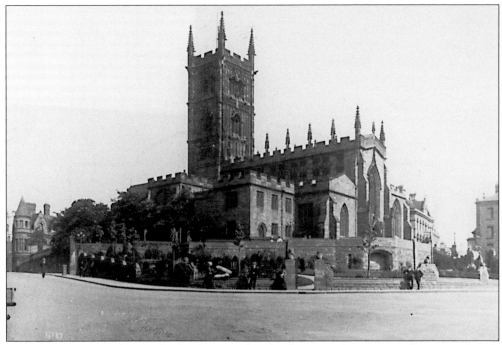

St Peter's Collegiate church, the focal point of Wolverhampton for over a millennium, though the existing building only dates from the fourteenth century. This view was only possible during the 1970s before the Civic Centre was built on the former market sites alongside.

An ornate flower arrangement in West Park in 1912, displaying the town's coat of arms including the motto 'Out of darkness cometh light'.

IMAGES
of England

WOLVERHAMPTON
A CENTURY OF CHANGE

Compiled by
Alec Brew

TEMPUS

First published 2000
Copyright © Alec Brew, 2000

Tempus Publishing Limited
The Mill, Brimscombe Port,
Stroud, Gloucestershire, GL5 2QG

ISBN 0 7524 2065 8

Typesetting and origination by
Tempus Publishing Limited
Printed in Great Britain by
Midway Clark Printing, Wiltshire

Acknowledgements

In the preparation of this book I turned once more to some of the stalwarts on whom I have come to rely during the compilation of my previous seven books on the town. Harry Blewitt's amazing collection of old postcards yielded at least forty I had never seen before. I used many more of David Clare's collection of photographs of most of the streets and buildings of the inner town, taken during the 1970s. Jim Boulton's esoteric collection of books, photographs and other artefacts also yielded many more wonderful images.

--The West Midland Aviation Archive, administered by the Boulton Paul Association, provided several photographs and not just of the town's aviation history. Miss A.M. Randle of Penn came up with nearly a dozen varied and interesting photographs, and Andy and Ray Simpson found me many more.

--Others I have to thank include Percy Kyte, John Parker, TRW Lucas Aerospace, and the extraordinarily patient Wendy Matthiason.

Contents

Acknowledgements   4

Introduction   7

1.   Before the Turn of the Century   9

2.   1901-1914   25

3.   The First World War   55

4.   1919-1939   61

5.   The Second World War   89

6.   1945-1960   99

7.   1960-1980   111

8.   1980-2000   123

The hub of Wolverhampton has always been Queen Square, known in centuries past as High Green. This view shows the square before the First World War, when the Lorain system trams were still running and the Empire Palace of Varieties (on the left) had not yet become the Hippodrome.

In 1963 diesel buses, like the Guy Arab in the foreground, were about to completely supplant the trolley bus, like the one behind. They are seen in Lichfield Street passing the Sir Tatton Sykes Hotel.

Introduction

During the twentieth century Wolverhampton celebrated its own Millennium; 1000 years since the town's foundation by Lady Wulfruna. However this is not a book about that long history, this collection of photographs seeks to show the changes wrought in the town during the last hundred years, and slightly earlier during the era of the camera. It is a record of some of the events that have shaped the town's history during that time, and affected the lives of Wulfrunians. I have found it impossible to illustrate all the events that have taken place in the town over the last century, two hundred photographs are just not enough!

Even when I was compiling the other seven books, illustrating each of the suburbs of the town, I found that two hundred photographs was not nearly enough to cover such a diverse and interesting community. I could not illustrate every pub, every school, every company, and every trophy won by the Wolves. All I could ever hope to do is give a flavour of what it was like to live in, and around Wolverhampton during the twentieth century. Although this book, more so than the others, features the 'great, the good, and the famous', it also aims to portray the lives of the ordinary people of Wolverhampton, in their schooling, work and their own back street.

Wolverhampton has always been a town split into two halves. The old debate about whether it was part of the Black Country, would have been instantly answered a hundred years ago by anyone walking down the Willenhall Road beyond Lower Horseley Fields, or through Monmore Green to Ettingshall. The surrounding area was all old coal mine workings and iron and steel industries, which were gathered along the Birmingham Canal; all very much part of the Black Country. Yet on the other side of the town centre, leafy avenues like the Penn Road and the Tettenhall Road stretched out into the countryside, though as the century progressed many small farming hamlets were engulfed by the expansion of the town, as new housing estates gobbled field after field.

The heavy engineering flavour of the town's industries has been tempered in more recent years by the closure of some of the old companies and their replacement with smaller, more high technology ones, symbolised by the establishment of the Science Park on the former Gas Works site, in partnership with the university.

The university has brought a revolution to the town centre's nightlife as well. The closure of all the old cinemas was threatening to make the centre a ghost town after dark, but the opening of many new theme pubs and night clubs within refurbished buildings which used to be banks, warehouses, shops, or indeed cinemas, has made the centre a exciting place to be at night. But then Wolverhampton always was!

Wolverhampton, a Century of Change, compiled by Alec Brew joins
a series of seven books by him on the suburbs of the town:

Codsall and Claregate
Tettenhall and Pattingham
Penn and Blakenhall
Ettingshall and Monnmore Green
Willenhall to Horseley Fields
Heath Town and Fallings Park
Bushbury and Featherstone

Also available in the Tempus Images of England Series:

Wolverhampton by Mary Mills and Tracey Williams
Bilston, Wednesfield and Tettenhall by Mary Mills and Tracey Williams
Staffordshire and Black Country Airfields by Alec Brew
Shropshire Airfields by Alec Brew and Barry Abraham
Albrighton and Shifnal by Alec Brew
Boulton Paul Aircraft by The Boulton Paul Association

The 'old and the new'; the peculiar
Victorian four-storey building on the
corner of Dudley Street and the former
St John's Street, has the office block of
the Mander Centre towering over it.
This photograph was taken in the last
year of the twentieth century from King
Street, which itself features untouched
Victorian buildings on one side, and new
concrete buildings on the other.

One

Before the Turn of the Century

As an historical date, 1 January 1901 may have been a significant turning point in the calendar, but across Wolverhampton, life merely went on as normal. A war was being fought in South Africa, involving soldiers from Wolverhampton; the Wolves were struggling in Division One, and the town council was planning the replacement of the horse-drawn trams with electric ones. All these things continued, just as they had done in the nineteenth century.

This chapter takes the opportunity to present a glimpse of what Wolverhampton was like at the start of the century, and how it had got there. This would be the century of the motor car; in 1901 three of the town's companies had already built powered vehicles, and many more would follow their example. Many of the institutions of the town were already in place, and it's important to consider their development.

Most importantly of all, many of the Wulfrunians who were to shape the town in the twentieth century were products of the Victorian age, and it is important to remember this. For instance the reason a huge Art & industrial Exhibition was planned at the beginning of the new century, was because two such events had already been successfully held in the town.

The town of Wolverhampton, as it appeared from West Park in the nineteenth century. St Peter's church is the dominant building on the skyline, and a century later the tower is still the highest point in the town. The park was opened in 1881 on the site of the town's racecourse on Broad Meadows.

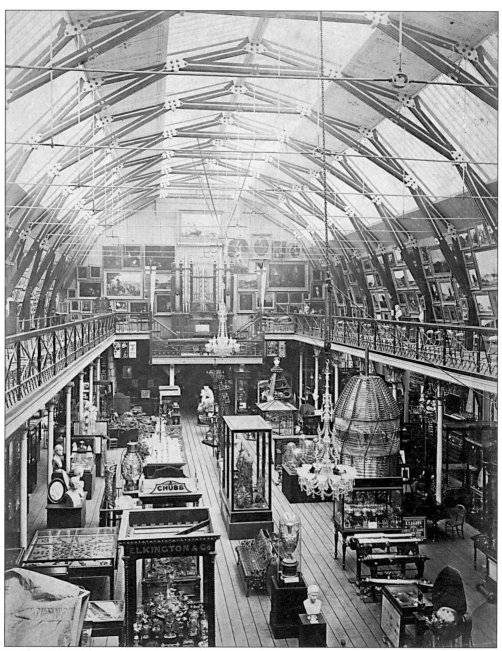

In 1869 Wolverhampton held the South Staffordshire Industrial and Fine Arts Exhibition in the grounds of Molineux House. This huge temporary hall was erected in the gardens of the House, which had recently been vacated by the Molineux family, and had become a hotel, with its grounds in use as pleasure gardens. Amongst the companies which can be seen exhibiting, are the Eagle Coal & Iron Company of West Bromwich, Elkington & Co, Chubb's, and E.F. Allen's Royal Music Salon of Queen Street. Artworks are on display in the galley.

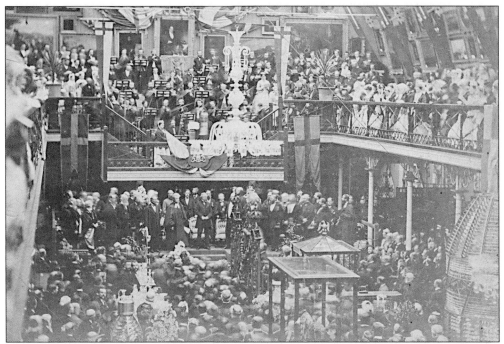

The grand opening of the exhibition was performed by Earl Granville on 11 May 1869, and most of the shopkeepers in the town closed for the morning, such was the interest in the event. It is interesting to note that where the band is playing behind the dignitaries in this picture, there is an organ sited in the previous picture.

The seventeenth-century Deanery House in Wulfruna Street. This beautiful large house was demolished in 1921, despite widespread opposition, in order to make way for the Wolverhampton and South Staffordshire Technical College, and the old site is now the main entrance to the University of Wolverhampton.

The art gallery and museum as it appeared at the end of the nineteenth century, having opened in 1884. It was largely paid for by Phillip Horseman, a gift commemorated by the fountain which was built alongside in St Peter's gardens. The cast iron railings to the gardens have recently been reinstated. The roof of Deanery House can be seen to the left.

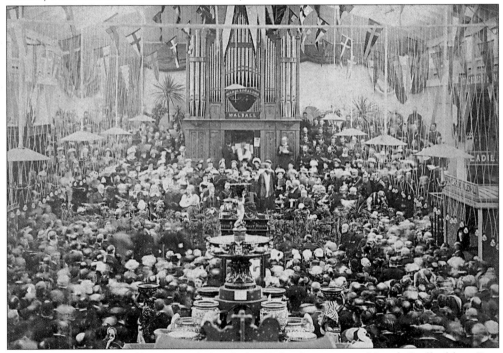

The opening of the art gallery coincided with the Wolverhampton and South Staffordshire Fine Arts and Industrial Exhibition of 1884, which was held inside. This is the opening ceremony in the gallery courtyard, near the rear entrance from Wulfruna Street, and dominated by the large pipe organ supplied by Nicholoson and the Lord of Walsall.

This photograph is something of a mystery. At first glance it appears to be a large crowd gathered in Lichfield Street, with the art gallery and St Peter's church in the background. However, a closer examination reveals the buildings to be a painted backdrop, and the balconies on either side appear to be of a temporary nature. There is a military band and some dignitaries on the stage in the background, and no other clue. It is clear though that the crowd appears to represent a sizeable portion of the middle class population of the town in the late nineteenth century.

The general post office, with Grand Theatre beyond, in Lichfield Street before the tram tracks were put down in 1902. The post office was opened in 1897 and the Grand in 1894, so the two buildings will have been almost new when this photograph was taken.

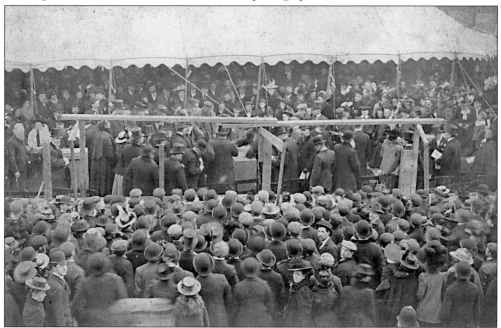

The laying of the foundation stone for Darlington Street Methodist church, 23 february 1900 by Sir Henry Fowler, MP. Unfortunately most of the crowd, in their assorted hats, have their backs to the camera. The church was opened in October 1901.

Typical of the quiet streets leading out of the town in the days before the motor car or even the tram. This shows the corner of Merridale Road and Compton Road, with the post office/telegraph office on the right in Compton Road. On the left is the Old Bell Inn, No. 15 Chapel Ash, with the Presbyterian church behind. The eye infirmary now sits on this corner.

The town of Wolverhampton regularly raised money to build lifeboats, and this is the *H.G. Powell* being launched at the Point of Ayre on 4 June 1896. Horatio Gibbs Powell, of Tettenhall, was on the Lifeboat Committee; many of the members travelled to attend the launch. From left to right: -?-, Thomas Williams, Samuel Hand (honourable secretary), T.P. Hadingham, Francis Hinde (vice-chairman),-?- , C. Powell, H.G. Powell, J.F. Steward, James Dodd, T.J. Barnett (treasurer), Herbert Wood, F.H. Skidmore,-?-.

St Andrew's church and Institute, Coleman Street, Whitmore Reans. This area of the town had been built in the nineteenth century, and was the first attempt at planned housing for the growing industrial workforce of Wolverhampton. St Andrew's was built in 1866, unfortunately it burned down in 1964, and was replaced by a new church. The institute was typical of many, providing the local people with more cultural interests.

The Wolverhampton Early Closing Association football team, for the season 1896-1997, played largely in the Rough Hills area of the town, towards Ettingshall. As the name suggests this was an area of abandoned coal workings and spoil heaps.

Wolverhampton Hockey Club in 1899. As half of the team have dark right-hand sides of their shirts, and the others white right-hand sides, one can assume that the shirts were created by cutting all-white and all-coloured shirts down the middle, and sewing the opposite halves together!

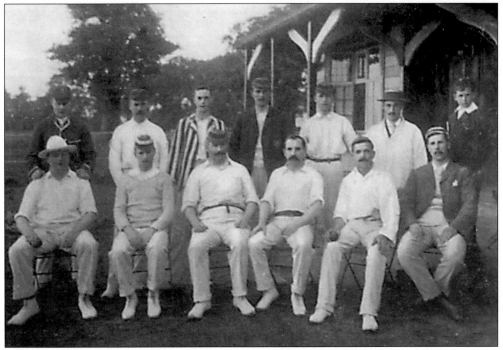

Wolverhampton Cricket Club in 1899, including the twelfth man, and a small boy on the pavilion balcony.

Messrs Richards' Beau Ideal bicycle factory in Railway Street, Heath Town around 1900. In that year there were over thirty bicycle manufacturers in Wolverhampton, six times as many as any other town or city in the country. Beau Ideal was not considered one of the Wolverhampton bicycle manufactures however, as Heath Town still had twenty-seven years of independence before it became part of Wolverhampton, although they did have showrooms in Gresham Street.

The 'new' generator factory at the Electric Construction Company in Bushbury, around 1900. ECC had been founded by 'Honest' Tom Parker and Bedford Elwell in 1880, and by 1898 was already making electric vehicles as well as electricity generating equipment of all kinds.

One of the shops of James Gibbons, St John's Works which was a large manufacturer of art metal work and high class locks. Like the neighbour Willenhall, Wolverhampton was well known for its lock-makers, of which Chubbs was the largest.

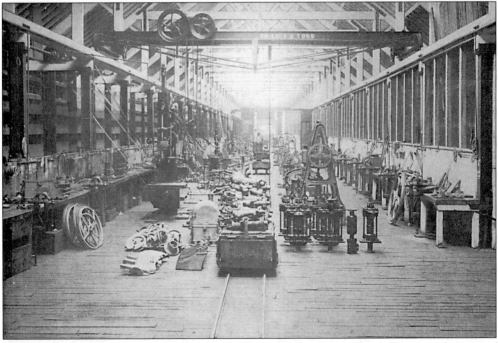

The interior of Joseph Evans' giant Culwell Works, Woden Road, Heath Town, at the turn of the twentieth century. The factory made pumps of all sizes, with parts coming from their own brass and iron foundries on the trucks on the central rails. The factory was typical of the heavy engineering factories in the area, but it closed just after the Second World War.

Penn was known as the leafy side of Wolverhampton, and this is where Harriet Sparrow founded St Catherine's Convalescent Home for women and children in 1871, being enlarged in 1889 to hold eighteen beds. The donkey-powered dogcart has featured on several photographs of the area.

Captain Morton's balloon, *Dudley Castle*, ascending from Molineux Gardens on 11 September 1882, with Col. Thorneycroft of Tettenhall as a passenger. Balloon flights were a fairly common attraction at this time, and this was one of a number starting from the Molineux. They landed at Smethwick an hour later, having flown little higher than the rooftops all the way because the balloon did not generate much lift.

A group of guests at Col. Thorneycroft's house, Tettenhall Towers. Tettenhall ridge was a popular place for the rich industrialists of Wolverhampton to live. Throneycroft's money came from iron and steel, as did that of his neighbours, the Hickman family. Also nearby were the Manders (paints and ink), John Marston (Sunbeam bicycles and cars) and Edward Lisle (Star bicycles and cars).

The Hall of Tettenhall Towers, showing the ornate style favoured by Col. Thorneycroft, who installed many of his own inventions in the building, including sock warmers integral with the central heating. The building is now part of Tettenhall College.

Wolverhampton Grammar School in St John's Lane, which ran from Dudley Street to Victoria Street. It had been founded on the site in 1512, and was to move to its present site in Merridale Road in 1890. St John's Lane is now part of the Mander Centre.

The laboratory of the Higher Grade School in Newhampton Road in 1896. Completed in 1894 the school offered a modern, practical secondary education. The Higher Grade School moved to Old Hall Street in 1921, and the Municipal Grammar School took over the Newhampton Road buildings.

Typical of the primary schools across the town was St Michael's in Lower Street, Tettenhall. At this time however, Tettenhall was not yet part of Wolverhampton, retaining its independence until 1967. This class group of girls dates from about 1896.

St Mary's church, Bushbury, founded about 1350 on a much older preaching site. In the last century Bushbury was a quiet backwater hamlet, though the parish itself was a large one, including Coven and Essington. It was not until the 1920s that Wolverhampton's expansion started to threaten its tranquillity, but it was not engulfed until the 1950s.

The carriage of the Duke and Duchess of York turning into Waterloo Road from Darlington Street on 23 July 1900. They had come to open the Jubilee Memorial Free Library and the new infirmary at the Royal Orphanage. Their progress from High Level Station continued down Bath Road to Chapel Ash, and back up Darlington Street to Snow Hill, then out to Penn after opening the library.

As the nineteenth century drew to a close in December 1900, Britain was at war in South Africa. This is the Service Company of the 3rd Staffordshire Volunteer Battalion, including many Wolverhampton men, off to fight the Boers.

Two

1901-1914

Though the twentieth century opened with the Empire at war in South Africa, by January 1901 there were signs that the army was at last winning that war. The British Empire stretched across the face of the globe and Wolverhampton and the other towns of the Black Country were the workshop of that Empire. There was every reason to look forward to the new century with eager anticipation. Wolverhampton's industry did not just involve heavy iron and steel products; some of the town's companies were at the cutting edge of technological achievement. The Electric Construction Company had built its first electric vehicles and both Star and Sunbeam had built their first motor cars. Such advances and the success of previous art and industrial exhibitions inspired a new one, far bigger and better than anything yet attempted outside London. The setting would be the beautifully matured West Park, and the town's new municipal transport system would ferry visitors from across the borough and from the two mainline railway stations. The new electric trams were of a revolutionary design, employing the Lorain surface contact system, so that the town's skyline would not need to be littered with overhead wires. By the time the new exhibition opened, the tracks were laid down Waterloo Road into Newhampton Road to disgorge thousands of visitors.

As the twentieth century began there was a huge sense of optimism in the town, typified by the construction of the large new Art and Industrial Exhibition in and around West Park. This is the Industrial Hall under construction in 1901. It was being built in the fields between the park and Newhampton Road.

Next to the Industrial Building, Canada had its own pavilion, and it is shown here, flags flying, ready for the exhibition opening in May 1902.

Though this view shows huge crowds milling around the large pavilions built alongside Newhampton Road; the exhibition was not to be a financial success, losing a large amount of money. To the right is the Industrial Hall, then the Canadian Pavilion, a concert hall, and the machinery hall.

Within the park the exhibition was more like a modern theme park, with this revolutionary water chute into the lake. Col. Thorneycroft was to try it out, but his car hit the water at the wrong angle, and he was badly injured. He never fully recovered and died the following year.

Other attractions included a huge spiral toboggan ride, swan boat rides on the lake, a miniature railway, and this maze which was called 'The House of Many Troubles'.

Newhampton Road, Wolverhampton. PUBLISHED BY C. SMITH

This view shows Newhampton Road after the exhibition had closed. The area has returned to normality, but the new tram tracks run towards Newbridge. The only traffic is a parked motor cycle and sidecar.

Snow Hill in 1905, with the statue of Sir Pelham Villiers (Wolverhampton's longest serving MP) on the right. The newly opened library, on the site of the former Theatre Royal, is to the rear, then the Corn Exchange Inn, advertising Butler's Ales, J.T. Pinson's sweet shop and Denton's Foundry, shortly to be supplanted by George Brown, the ironmonger.

Opposite the library and behind Sir Pelham, was the Agricultural Hall, 1905. The hall was built in 1863, and as the name suggests, served as a corn exchange and for the sale of other farming products, but was also used as a concert hall and meeting place. It was later turned into a large cinema, and after being demolished was the site of the Gaumont Palace cinema.

Billingham Bros's cycle shop, Nos 430-431 Dudley Road, showing a huge amount of stock. Billingham's later became one of the town's main car dealers, and occupied George Brown's ironmonger's building opposite the Agricultural Hall in 1911.

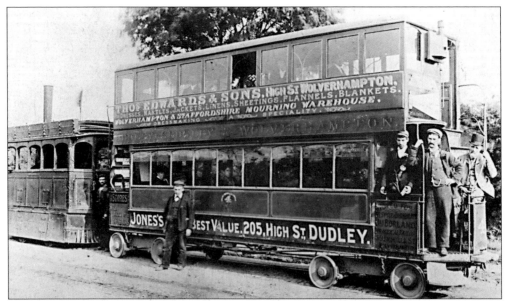

A steam hauled tramcar, which was used by the Dudley & Wolverhampton Company for a while at the beginning of the twentieth century.

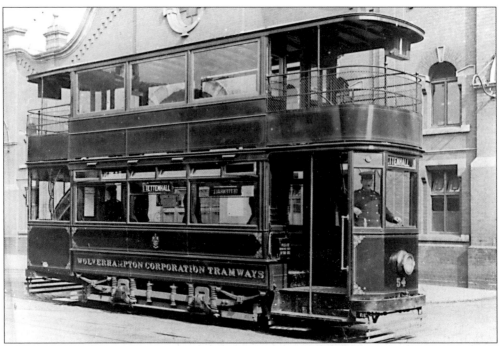

A Wolverhampton Corporation tram outside the municipal depot on Cleveland Road. This one is about to set out on Route No. 1 to Tettenhall. The Lorain surface contact system was always looked upon with suspicion, but stories of horses being electrocuted through their iron shoes have never been proven.

A tram passes down Lichfield Street into Prince's Square, heading for the Bilston Road around 1904. Price-Lewis, the tailors, occupied the Royal Exchange building on the right.

One of the first motor-buses used in Wolverhampton, a Wolseley, No. DA110. The Wolseleys were used to travel to the new, growing suburb of Penn Fields, from 1905-1909 when the tram tracks were finally laid on the route.

Dudley Street, always the main shopping street in the town, and always treated as if it was pedestrianized, even before it really was. H. Samuel's can be seen in the background, on the corner of Queen Street where it still stands today.

Wolverhampton's magnificent Central Arcade, an indoor shopping 'mall'. This one ran from Dudley Street to St John's Lane. The other arcade, the Queen's, was in a cul-de-sac off Queen Square.

Snow Hill, with Clarkson's furniture store, a feature of the town for most of the century, occupying Nos 48 and 49. A little further along, Snow Hill Post Office can be seen behind the little boy.

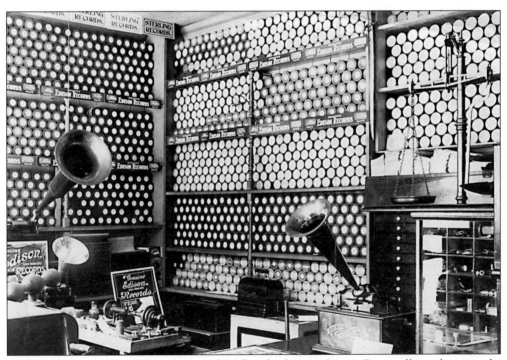

'Those are funny CDs!' The interior of Redhead's shop in Piper's Row, selling phonographs and cylinders, with Edison Records and Sterling Records advertised. The use for the scales is not known.

The grinders and polishers at the Chillington Tool Company in 1906. Chillington Tool was a large producer of agricultural implements in Hickman Avenue, Horsley Fields, and was especially famous for its 'Crocodile' brand tools.

The magnificent wholesale market building, to the right, which was opened in 1903, facing many of its customers in the retail markets.

The Wolverhampton Fire Brigade who were based in Red Lion Street, having been set up as a twelve man force in 1853.

As the century progressed, Wolverhampton became one of the major motor manufacturing towns in the country. Leading the way was the Star Engineering Company on Frederick Street, run by the Lisle family. This is a Star 80hp at Wightwick in 1903, with Sir Alfred Hickman being driven by Joseph Lisle.

Molineux gardens became famous for cycle races in the last years of the nineteenth century, and this even continued after Wolverhampton Wanderers made it their home in 1889. The famous 'cow-shed' stand can be seen to the left.

West Park, Wolverhampton

In 1908 West Park with its linked lakes remained the town's premier park. The equally large East Park had been completed in 1893, but by 1906 had lost its lake, which drained away into the old mine workings beneath. East Park never had a magnificent conservatory like West Park's, seen to the left of this picture.

One feature of West Park which is no l
onger apparent, is 'The Dingle', a pathway
constructed by a small waterfall into the lake.

THE DINGLE, WEST PARK, WOLVERHAMPTON

The Keep, Dunstall Hall, Wolverhampton.

The keep was a folly built in Dunstall Park
by James Hordern, who acquired Dunstall
Hall in 1818. The property came into the
hands of Alexander Staveley who sold the
park to create a new racecourse in 1887.
The town had been without a racecourse for
nine years since Broad Meadows was turned
into West Park. The Hall and keep were
demolished in 1916, and the adjoining lake
filled in.

The start of North Street in 1910, with the Town Hall in the background. The Empire Palace of Varieties theatre is just to the right, and the Staffordshire Knot is prominent on the seed store next door.

Lichfield Street in 1910, with Price-Lewis, the tailors still trading from the Royal Exchange Building to the right, and the Metropolitan Bank between that and the art gallery.

QUEEN SQUARE. WOLVERHAMPTON. 432

Queen Square pictured sometime after 1921, when the Empire Palace had become the Hippodrome, and the Lorain system trams had been replaced by the more normal overhead contact system. The Hippodrome became a cinema for one year after the Agricultural Hall was demolished and before the Gaumont was built, but then returned to being a theatre. In the background is the Queen's Picture House.

Wolverhampton. Chapel Ash.

The lower end of Chapel Ash in the very early years of the twentieth century, when the Lorain trams were running to Tettenhall, but there were no motor cars to be seen. The building at the junction of Compton Road and Tettenhall Road is still there, as is the building on the right.

Further along the Tettenhall Road the Half Way House can be seen to the right on the corner of Paget Road. It is half way between London and Holyhead. Apart from the tram, the horse-drawn wagon, and the height of the trees, this scene is very similar today.

Lower Street Tettenhall around 1912, then just inside the Tettenhall Borough boundary. The cottages on the left and the Swan public house in the background are still there, but the houses on the right have gone.

A large crowd milling around on the Upper Green, Tettenhall, some time before the clock tower was built in 1911. Being at the end of a tram route, Tettenhall was popular for a day out for the people of Wolverhampton, wishing to enjoy its leafier surroundings.

Rock Hotel, Tettenhall. Bowling Green, A close en

One of the popular destinations in Tettenhall was the Rock Hotel, and its bowling green. This picture shows a close end being measured during a game in 1910.

The tool department of the Electric Construction Company in Bushbury in 1908. One of the largest employers in the town, ECC continued to make electrical generating equipment until its closure in the 1980s.

Hardly Formula 1! Dick Lisle in a 12 hp Star racer outside the Frederick Street factory. This car was the first streamlined car to race at Brooklands. Star had competed in motoring competitions from 1900, but entered their first real race in 1903, and were particularly successful on the Brooklands track.

A presentation at Dunstall Park on 8 August 1908, where a fete was being held. Standing is L.S. Amery who had recently lost a by-election in the town, standing as an Unionist. He lost by just eight votes to the Liberal candidate, Ald. George Thorne. On Amery's left is Sir Alfred Hickman, and then Staveley Hill. On his other side is Mr Bird, of Bird's Custard, who was at the time a prospective Conservative Party candidate for Wolverhampton West.

Darlington Street in 1910, showing the Methodist church, opposite the Wolverhampton gas company's offices on the corner of Waterloo Road. St Mark's church, Chapel Ash, is in the distance.

The Royal Hospital, which had opened as the South Staffordshire Hospital & Dispensary in 1849, and after many extensions and additions had, by the time this photograph was taken, become the Wolverhampton & Staffordshire General Hospital. It did not become the 'Royal' until 1928.

A huge crowd gathered in Queen Square on 19 May 1910 for the proclamation of King George V.

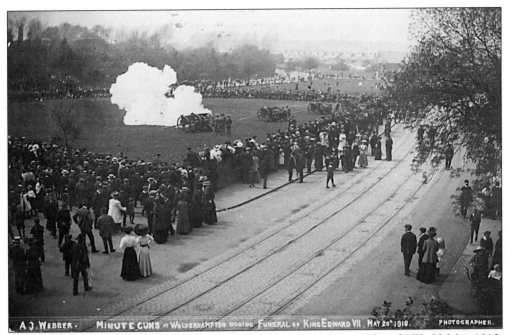

A minute gun fires a salute on the occasion of the funeral of King Edward VII, 20 May 1910. The guns are in the fields between Newhampton Road and West Park, where the 1902 exhibition had been held.

A photograph of the same corner of Newhampton Road, from the opposite direction, taken on 25 August 1911, as local Territorial Army soldiers depart for London, to take part in the coronation of King George V.

45

Part of the ceremonies to inaugurate the new improvements and open spaces to the west of St Peter's church on 13 June 1907.

Ornate flower arrangements were a feature of the centre of West Park for many years, and for the Coronation of King George V this elegant crown is being transported to the middle of the central circular bed, where it would become one of the most photographed attractions ever seen in the park.

A view along Dudley Street towards Snow Hill, with a tram about to pass the Agricultural Hall. This whole section of street was completely blocked by the construction of the Wulfrun Shopping Centre in the 1970s.

Queen Square in 1913, with the town's wheeled fire-fighting ladder parked in its usual place next to Prince Albert's statue. The Board public house advertises 'Harmer Ales' in between the Midland Cafe and the famous old Wolverhampton institution, Reynolds Restaurant. The Board had recently switched from Lawrence Ales because Mr Lawrence had spent all his money defending himself in a murder trial.

St Luke's church, Upper Villiers Street, Blakenhall. The church was built, unusually, in ornate brickwork rather than stone, and opened in 1860.

The Penn Road, and though actually taken long after the war when the trolley bus had replaced the tram, it otherwise would have looked very much like this in 1913. Later of course it became the most congested suburban road in the country.

Coalway Road in Penn Fields, typical of the suburban sprawl which engulfed the area to the west of Wolverhampton, beginning in the mid-nineteenth century and continuing as far as the borough boundary at Penn Common.

St Phillips church, Penn Fields, one of the churches built for the increasing population of the area. The girl leaning on the gatepost was one of the daughters of Mr Keay of Coalway Farm. This was one of the farms which was engulfed by the new expansion.

In June 1910 the first ever All-British Flying Meeting was held by the newly formed Midland Aero Club on Dunstall Park Racecourse. The two previous flying meetings in 1909 had been dominated by French flyers. Eleven of the sixteen holders of British Aviator's Certificates flew at the meeting, including Claude Grahame White (centre) and James Radley (capless). They are no doubt discussing the appalling weather which dogged the week's flying.

Another entry was Alan Boyle in his Avis Monoplane, designed by the foremost British aircraft designers of the day, Howard and Warwick Wright, both born in Dudley. In the background, Great Western Railway men have a grandstand view of the flying from the vantage point of Oxley Sidings.

The Bushury Scout Troop at High Level Station, giving a send off to Joe Driffield, brother of the scout leader, Horace, in 1911. High Level Station, Wolverhampton's first main station, was at that time completely covered over with a fine roof.

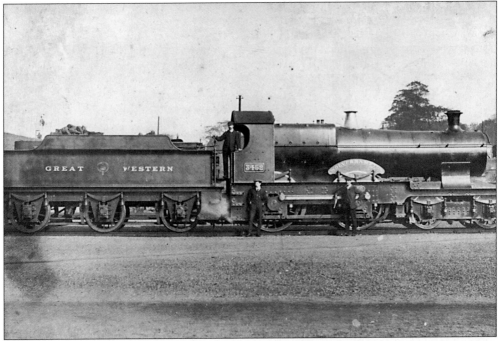

Wolverhampton was a 'railway town' with the GWR's Stafford Road works building engines, and several different companies' lines criss-crossing the town. This is the GWR 'Bulldog' Class locomotive named 'Wolverhampton' outside Stafford Road works, though it was built in Swindon. Tom Wedge, standing in front of the number plate, worked in the Stafford Road offices.

Trinity Methodist church on the Compton Road was built in 1862, largely through the generosity of the Thorneycroft family. It was one of only four Methodist churches in England which also hosted Anglican services, but was demolished in 1976. The Quarter House Inn is in the foreground where a couple of waggoners have stopped for a quick one!

William Butler moved his successful brewing operation to the Springfield Brewery in 1874, and widely delivered his ales in the West Midlands. Here is his first motor lorry, outside the Crystal Fountain Inn, Cannock.

PARK ROAD, WOLVERHAMPTON.

Park Avenue ran all the way around West Park, and in 1911 when this picture was taken, there were very few houses on the opposite side of the road. These are between Park Avenue, which emerges in the background, and Park Crescent, which ran to Bath Road. They are all still there, though these and many of the other villas, subsequently built round the park, have been turned into flats.

WOLVERHAMPTON YEOMANRY GOING TO CAMP

The Territorial Army drill hall, between Newhampton Road and Park Avenue, with the Wolverhampton Yeomanry emerging to go on one of their annual camps. The camps were a great inducement to join, as they were looked on by the local working man as a holiday away from the toil and grime of their normal lives.

John Marston began making motor cycles in 1911, in Sunbeamland, where his bicycles were made. His Sunbeam cars were from 1905 made by a separate company in the Moorfield Works. This is the Sunbeam team which won the team prize in their first ever Isle of Man Senior T.T Race in 1914. From left to right: R. Tommy de la Hay, Vernon Busby, Howard Davies, Charlie Nokes. Howard Davies came second overall. The junior race was won by the AJS team from a little further along the Penn Road.

The Sunbeam Motor Car Co. began making aero engines in 1912, and bought in this Farman biplane to test fly their 150hp V8 side valve engine. In the pilot's seat is Jack Alcock whom they engaged as test pilot. In 1919, Jack and Arthur Whitten Brown, became the first men to fly the Atlantic non-stop. A few months after this picture was taken Alcock was in uniform, and the aircraft had been impressed into service.

Three

The First World War

At the outbreak of the First World War there was a rush to join the services, but many of the working people of Wolverhampton were better employed producing the goods and equipment with which to fight the war. The town's vehicle manufacturers, like Star, Sunbeam, Clyno, AJS, and the newly formed Guy Motors, found ready markets with the military for their cars, motor cycles and trucks, and as the war progressed, more and more of the industry of the town was turned over to the manufacture of munitions.

The small pre-war beginnings of Sunbeam in the aero-engine business was to pay off with large orders for their V8 and V12 engines, which were the only British aero-engines of high power in existence in 1914. They were also to accept large orders for Shorts and Avro aeroplanes, so that production of their cars, much in demand for staff transport, was turned over to Rover in Coventry. Star produced wings for the Avro 504s which Sunbeam built, and near the end of the war accepted large orders for aero-engines, as did Clyno and Guy Motors.

Wolverhampton was to escape the Zeppelin and Gotha raids which were to create headlines elsewhere, though the damage they caused was exaggerated. On the whole the Zeppelin crews had not the faintest idea where they were or what they were bombing, so if they hit anything vital it was more by luck than judgement.

Amy Emms, aged two, outside her grandmother's shop, No. 72, All Saints Road, in 1914. The newspaper posters ask 'Can we save Serbia?' and 'Britain in the Balkans, why we went'. Similar questions were to be asked eighty years later.

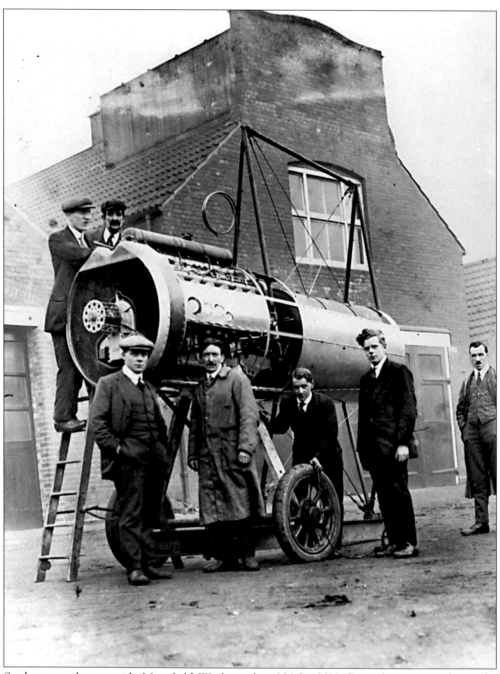

Sunbeam workers outside Moorfield Works with a 320 hp V12 Cossack engine and nacelle, ready for installation in a Handley Page O/400 heavy bomber. O/400s were being made just down the road at the Birmingham Carriage Works in Handsworth.

Rows of Sunbeam Arab 200 hp V8 aero-engines ready for despatch in the Moorfield Works in 1918. In the background can be seen some 260hp V12 Maori engines.

Inside H.M. Hobson's Accuracy Works in Cousins Street during the war. Hobson's produced the Claudel-Hobson carburettors which were to prove vital to the war effort. A large proportion of the town's workforce were now women, taking over the jobs of the men who had gone to the Front.

Sunbeam produced just one aircraft of its own design during the war, the Sunbeam Bomber, shown here ready for delivery on Castle Bromwich airfield. It was not ordered into production.

Sunbeam workers busy themselves around the Sunbeam Bomber. The man in the middle, slightly hidden, is Louis Coatalen, the Frenchman who became Sunbeam's chief engineer in 1909, and was to have a controlling influence over all its products.

The fuselages of Avro 504 trainers lined up outside the Moorfield Works, being delivered, two per truck load. The Star Engineering Company built the wings, and between them the two companies built 541 Avros by the time orders were cancelled after the war.

A captured 77mm German gun displayed next to Prince Albert's statue in Queen Square during 'Gun Week' when £920,000 was raised in Great Britain for the war effort. The gun had been captured at the Battle of Loos by the 15th Division.

A float, depicting 'Autumn' created by the workers of the Electric Construction Company for a parade on 28 September 1918.

The Victory Day celebrations in Coleman Street, Whitmore Reans. The long ordeal was over!

Four

1919-1939

With the return of peace the town struggled to return to normality. Orders for munitions and other war supplies were cancelled, and companies had to return to their former work, or find new products to sell. The Sunbeam took back their car production from Rover, but tried to stay in the aero-engine business, which had grown so large during the war.

The optimism felt at the beginning of the century returned now that 'The war to end all wars' was over. However emotions were also tinged with a weariness and sadness for all the lives that had been lost The erection of war memorials took place at many companies, and in most districts. The annual service on Armistice Day became a new institution. Wolverhampton was soon to engage on the construction of a house building programme in the Low Hill area, to provide 'Homes fit for heroes', but the first priority for many of the returning men was to be finding, and keeping, a job.

During the war Sunbeam had a large business providing power cars for airships, large and small, and this was to continue for a short while afterwards. This is the starboard forward car, complete with its 320 hp Sunbeam Cossack engine for the R38 Airship, the biggest British airship at that time. It was sold to the Americans and became the ZR2, but on acceptance trials it broke up over the Humber and caught fire, with great loss of life. A more successful Sunbeam-powered airship was the R34, the first airship to cross the Atlantic, and the first craft to fly both ways.

As part of the Wolverhampton hospitals carnival immediately after the war, Guy Motors built this large float as a hospital ship with employees dressed as the crew as well as the wounded and nurses. One person, dressed as a skeleton, looks too far gone for treatment!

ECC's entry in the same parade was with this ambulance team. The 'patient' was Tom Hall, the 'stretcher bearers' were Aaron Butler, Charlie Evans, William Hughes and Jack Price, and the 'nurse' was Ethel Beady.

Wolverhampton Town Hall after the war, with motor cars and motor cycles becoming common sights in the streets. This was actually the fifth town hall, and construction was completed in 1871. Now of course there is a sixth, grandly re-named the Civic Centre, and the old building has now been occupied by the Magistrates Courts.

To prove that art and sport can mix, or that sport is art, this is the Wolverhampton School of Art and Design Football team in 1920-1921.

A busy Chapel Ash in the 1920s, with the familiar Charles Clark & Sons showrooms on the left, advertizing themselves as agents for Austin, Star, Rover, Wolseley and Talbot cars. Charles Clark are still in Chapel Ash, though in a different building, and are still agents for Rover, and by default Wolseley and Austins.

Lichfield Street in the 1920s, with the Victoria Hotel on the left, and the Grand Theatre beyond it. The fine Victorian buildings opposite were all demolished to make way for the Co-op department store, which closed in the 1980s.

64

Queen Square from the top of a busy Darlington Street. James Beattie's Department store which began as a single shop in Victoria Street has already spread down Darlington Street, but the disparate premises had not yet been rebuilt into their current singular form.

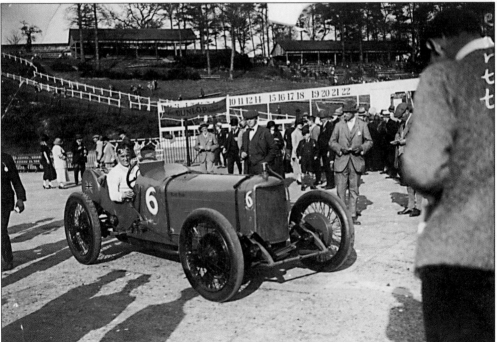

With the coming of peace, Louis Coatalen, the chief engineer of Sunbeam turned his thoughts towards racing once more, and in particular his ambition to win the French Grand Prix, which he achieved in 1923. This is Malcolm Campbell in a Sunbeam racing car in the paddock at Brooklands.

WOLVERHAMPTON WANDERERS' F.C. Season 1925-26

BRADLEY. GREGORY. BRADFORD. FOX. GEORGE. HAMPTON. CHARNLEY. WATSON. HOMER. LEES.

J.DAVIS. HIGHAM. BOSWELL. SHAW. KAY. O'CONNOR. CADDICK. McDOUGALL. SCOTT. TIMMINS. TAYLOR. G.HOLLEY.
(ASSIST.TRAINER)   (TRAINER)

LEGGE. BOWEN. KERR. HARRINGTON. TYLER. MITTON. PHILLIPSON. KEETLEY. PRICE. A.H.HOSKINS.
(SECRETARY).

Copyright. A.H.Poulton, Wolverhampton.   Photo by Arcade Studios. Wolverhampton.

The Wolverhampton Wanderers team for season 1925-1926, when they were in the 2nd Division, and finished 4th. From left to right, back row: Bradley, Gregory, Bradford, Fox, George, Hampton, Charnley, Watson, Homer, Lees. Middle row: J. Davis (assistant trainer), Higham, Bowell, Shaw, Hay, O'Connor, Caddick, McDougall, Scott, Timmins, Taylor, G. Holley (trainer) Front row: Legge, Bowen, Kerr, Harrington, Tyler, Mitton, Phillipson, Keetley, Price, A.H. Hoskins (secretary).

Wolves in action against Manchester United on 9 September 1922. Mew, the United goalkeeper, is saving from McMillan, the Wolves No. 7. Wolves lost the match 1-0 in what was a disastrous season. They finished bottom of Division 2 and were relegated, the lowest point in their fortunes until their spectacular dive to the 4th Division in the 1980s.

The Metropolitan Works Band at the Molineux in January 1925, for a community singing concert. Stirring renditions of popular favourites were on the agenda, perhaps to take peoples' minds off the hard times of the day.

Motor cycle outings were a popular recreation in the 1920s, with a number of clubs attached to major companies. This is believed to be the AJS works outing to the Dudley Arms Hotel.

Other Wulfrunians were more energetic, and belonged to cycling clubs. This one is gathering at the Mermaid Inn on the Bridgnorth Road ready to start a trip into the Shropshire countryside. Cycling clubs thought nothing of day trips to Wales.

Trips further afield were in the ubiquitous charabanc and this outing for the domestic staff is departing from the rear of Hilton Hall in 1926. It was driving just such a charabanc that Don Everall was to first make his name in the town.

The Scouting and Girl Guides Associations provided another opportunity for people to get away from the grime and poor air of the Black Country. These are scout and girl-guide leaders from Wolverhampton at a camp on Cannock Chase.

There was fierce rivalry between Wolverhampton's various motor cycle manufacturers on the racing circuits. This is the triumphant AJS team for the 1921 Isle of Man TT Races. From left to right: H.F. Harris, H.R. Davies (also competitions manager) Eric Williams. AJS were 1st, 2nd, 3rd and 4th in the Junior TT, with Williams 1st and Davies 2nd. Then Davies won the Senior TT on his 350cc Junior bike.

Howard Davies left AJS and formed his own company, HRD Motor-cycles, in 1924, firstly in Heath Town, and then in Fryer Street Wolverhampton. In their first TT in 1925, Davies was 2nd in the Junior TT with H.F. Harris 5th on another HRD, separated by two AJS riders, and Davies won the Senior TT. There were big celebrations in Wolverhampton on their return after two years of TT victories by Birmingham bikes. This is the HRD Depot on the Isle of Man in 1926, with H.R. Davies in front of the letter 'C'.

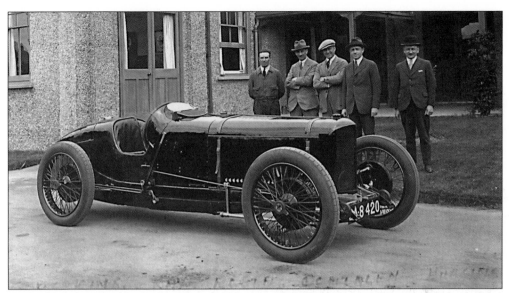

A Sunbeam two-litre racing car outside the company canteen in 1922. From left to right: Perkins (mechanic), C.B. Kay (works manager), Dario Resta (racing driver), Louis Coatalen (chief engineer) and General Huggins (director).

The Sunbeam 350 hp, later named Bluebird, on Pendine Sands in 1925, where Malcolm Campbell drove it to the World Land Speed Record, the first to exceed 150 mph. This car which had had aerodynamic improvements after work done in Boulton & Paul's wind tunnel in Norwich, is now in the National Motor Museum at Beaulieu.

A portion of the pupils in the Higher Grade School in 1921, with the headmaster in the centre. The school was by then in Old Hall Street, which is now the headquarters of the adult college.

Girls of the Upper Fifth playing tennis at Wolverhampton Girls High School in the late 1920s. It was jointly founded in 1911 by Staffordshire and Wolverhampton Councils, and originally took ninety girls from each. From 1927 the number from Staffordshire was reduced to a third of the intake. The girl on the left, Edith Baron, came from Pattingham, over the border in Staffordshire.

A busy Queen Square in the 1920s, with Prince Albert on his horse facing the often remembered underground lavatories. The Board public house, next to J. Lyons, was by now renamed the Shakespeare, and would later be called the Talk of the Town.

Henry Segrave in the 4 litre Sunbeam Tiger on Southport sands where he broke Sunbeam's own Land Speed Record, achieving 152 mph for the flying kilometre in March 1926.

Queen Mary's car driving into Wolverhampton along the Tettenhall Road on 22 March 1939 after visiting Lady Mander at Wightwick.

The Prince of Wales, later King Edward VIII, striding across the market place on 13 June 1923, with the mayor in tow. He had visited the Wolverhampton & Staffordshire General Hospital and presented a Royal Charter of Incorporation to the Hospital Board and Medical Staff, establishing the hospital as a legally constituted body.

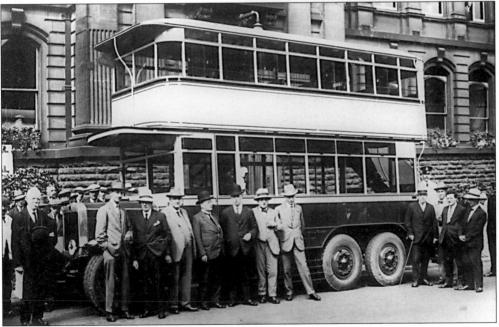

Guy Motors of Fallings Park established itself as one of the country's premier producers of buses. This is Britain's first six-wheeled double decker bus, (one of many of Guy's firsts) being handed over to Wolverhampton Council outside the town hall in 1926.

AJS were most famous for their motor-cycles but this was an AJS factory producing wirelesses, gramophones and loudspeakers in 1925. It was in Stewart Street, in a factory formerly used to build Briton cars.

The third Sunbeam Land Speed Record breaking car under test in the Moorfield Works' experimental department. The '1000hp Sunbeam' was powered by two 450hp aero engines, and became the first car in the world to exceed 200mph, on Daytona Beach in 1927.

An interesting collection of the works of 'Bill Posting', believed to be alongside the Tettenhall Road. Apart from the period advertisements, it shows that there were three theatres in competition, The Hippodrome, the Grand and the Theatre Royal, and just round the corner the West End Cinema (Worcester Street) advertises *Mademoiselle of Armentieres*.

Wolverhampton had its own country dancing club in the 1920s, and here the Wulfruna Folk Dance Group is giving a display of Morris Dancing in 1928. Second from the left is Ben Randle.

The church was often the centre of the local social scene, and here members of the congregation at St Chad's, Lime Street, Penn Fields, pose for a picture in 1928.

A Wolverhampton fire engine being used to carry the coffin of David Webster, the chief constable of Wolverhampton, in the late 1920s. They are moving away from St Peter's church, and both firemen and police lined the route with large crowds gathered to watch. At this time the fire department was under the jurisdiction of the police.

The workshop of the Blind Institute on Waterloo Road, with wicker laundry baskets being made. Sidney Wood, the workshop manager is standing in the centre, wearing a brown overall.

The staff of the Blind Institute gathered for a photograph in the late 1920s.

Sunbeam's last attempt on the World Land Speed Record was with the Silver Bullet, powered by two specially built supercharged engines. Here workers from the experimental department gather for a photograph before the car was shipped to Daytona Beach in March 1930. The attempt was dogged by technical difficulties and poor beach conditions, and they failed in their attempt to become the first car to exceed 250mph.

A view along Queen Street, from Dudley Street, with H. Samuel's in its familiar location on the corner. Next door is 'Hollywood Hats' a reminder of the time when every man wore a hat.

A view across Queen Square towards St Peter's. On the central island are the underground lavatories, well remembered in the town but now of course long gone.

The interior of St Peter's Collegiate church. The present building dates from 1425, but was built on the site of the original church endowed by Lady Wulfruna, who founded the town of Wolverhampton over 1,000 years ago.

The opening of a new putting green outside the clubhouse of Penn Golf Club, by the mayor, Councillor Morris Christopher, on 13 July 1935. There had been a golf club on Penn Common since the nineteenth century.

The celebration of King George V's Silver Jubilee in 1935, at the Wednesfield Cottage Homes, an event celebrated across the town, though at the time Wednesfield was still independent and remained so until 1967.

The Parade of the Midland clergy through Wolverhampton from St Peter's church on 24 June 1933. The procession took twenty minutes to pass.

A typical scene of Black Country industry seen in an aerial view of Alfred Hickman's Steelworks at Bilston in 1934, by then Stewart's & Lloyd's. Like Wednesfield, Bilston was at that time independent, but was swallowed up by Wolverhampton in 1967. The steelworks, 'ickman's as it was known, symbolised 'the Fiery Holes of the Black Country.'

Like most towns struggling out of the depression of the early 1930s, Wolverhampton desperately tried to attract new industries, and this small display in the town hall in 1936 illustrated the success stories of this policy. Goodyear's, Boulton Paul Aircraft, Courtauld's and the German company, Fischer Bearings are all apparent, as well as other companies which made springs, weights and measures and dominoes!

The Norwich Company of Boulton & Paul sold off its aircraft department in 1934 and Wolverhampton offered the independent Boulton Paul Aircraft a 'green field site' at Pendeford for its new factory. They were also offered one hundred years flying rights at the brand new airport. Here a Boulton Paul Overstrand stands in the flight shed at Pendeford in 1938. It has had its front turret removed to be replaced by an experimental mounting for a 20mm Hispano cannon.

In the 1920s Wolverhampton had undertaken a huge new housing project on Low Hill to replace the old Victorian slums. This project was linked to the integrated public transport system, featuring the new trolley buses. Here a Guy six-wheel trolley bus stands waiting at the Bushbury Hill Terminus around 1932.

Boulton Paul's first production aircraft at Pendeford was the Hawker Demon. Here examples of the 105 that they built stand ready for flight testing outside the new factory.

Like many towns in the country in the 1930s, Wolverhampton became 'air-minded', and built a municipal airport on land at Barnhurst Farm, a site selected by Sir Alan Cobham. The Midland Aero Club were invited to operate out of this new airport, as well as still using their home airport at Castle Bromwich. Here, the Mayor, Councillor R.E. Probert looks suitably aeronautical, standing by the club's first Tiger Moth.

Although flying began from Pendeford in 1936 the official opening was 25 June 1938, when a flying display took place. The small clubhouse/terminal, and a single hangar can be seen behind some of the aircraft gathered for the event.

One of the guests invited to the opening was the famous 'aviatrix' Amy Johnson, seen here striding from the hangar.

To many Wulfrunians, the year 1939 is remembered for two disasters, the outbreak of the Second World War and the unexpected defeat of the Wolves in the FA Cup Final by Portsmouth. Here the captain Stan Cullis, introduces the team to his Majesty King George VI. Despite his appearance, Cullis was only twenty-two, and had already played for England nine times.

With war clouds looming, the Boulton Paul factory is being camouflaged; the painter can be seen on the shortest of his three ladders. Outside the flight-sheds are a line of Blackburn Roc naval fighters. Boulton Paul built all one hundred and thirty-six Rocs.

Five

The Second World War

For the second time in the twentieth century, Wolverhampton was to gear itself up for war, turning over its metal-bashing industries to the production of munitions. Some companies were already involved in the build up of the armed forces when war began. Boulton Paul had two production lines of two seat fighters, the Roc and its own Defiant. As the war progressed, Goodyear were turning out tyres for the military Guy Motors' armoured cars and trucks, Henry Meadows the engines, John Thompsons the new-fangled landing craft Ever Ready military wirelesses, and GKN the nuts and bolts to hold them all together.

Everyday life was to change dramatically, as rationing came into effect, gas masks needed to be carried everywhere, and the dreaded air-raid siren sent people scurrying down air raid shelters. With no street lights, and windows covered with black-out curtains, even walking home could be a dangerous task with the risk of colliding with lamp-posts, tripping over kerbs, and falling into bomb craters. Even those who were in reserved occupations, or were too old to fight, pulled on uniforms for the ARP, the volunteer fire departments or the Home Guard.

A line of Boulton Paul Defiants awaiting delivery outside the Pendeford factory. Some of these very five aircraft served with No. 264 Squadron over Dunkirk, and in the Battle of Britain.

Just north of the town, the Wolverhampton company of Sir Alfred MacAlpine & Sons, was building a new Royal Air Force Technical Training Station as the war began. RAF Cosford was also to be the home of No. 9 Maintenance Unit, storing RAF aircraft in these turf-covered concrete hangars. The close links between Wolverhampton and RAF Cosford have continued with the station being given the Freedom of the Borough.

As war progressed the Boulton Paul factory was expanded, and the new gun turret factory can be seen in this aerial view being frantically camouflaged. A Defiant night fighter sits outside one of the two Bellman hangars supplied by the Air Ministry, to the left. Note the fleet of buses on the other side of the canal, which were needed for a workforce which expanded to nearly 5,000.

Wolverhampton Municipal Airport was taken over by the RAF as the home for No. 28 Elementary Flying Training School, and a large new camp and four extra hangars were built. In the bottom right hand corner the taxiway to Boulton Paul's factory can be seen, running by six blast pens cut into the hillside where aircraft could be parked.

The 108 Tiger Moths on charge with No. 28 EFTS were looked after by a private company, Air Schools Ltd, and this is the 400 hour inspection team, in front of one of their charges.

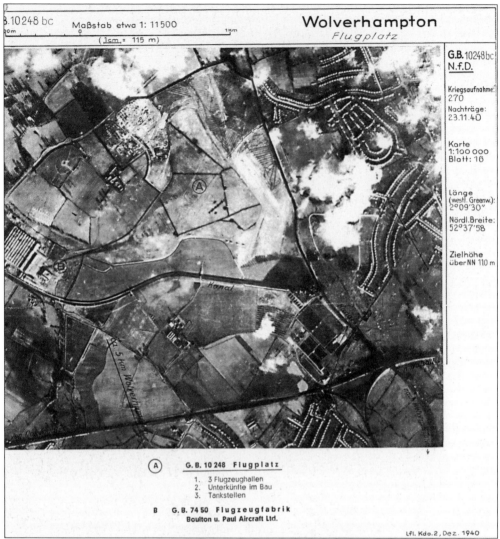

G.B.10248bc
N.f.D.

Kriegsaufnahme:
270
Nachträge:
23.11.40

Karte
1:100 000
Blatt: 16

Länge
(westl. Greenw.):
2°09'30"

Nördl.Breite:
52°37'58

Zielhöhe
überNN 110 m

Ⓐ   G.B. 10 248 Flugplatz

1. 3 Flugzeughallen
2. Unterkünfte im Bau
3. Tankstellen

B   G.B. 74 50 Flugzeugfabrik
     Boulton u. Paul Aircraft Ltd.

Lfl. Kdo.2, Dez. 1940

Despite the airfield being well camouflaged, with 'hedges' and 'trees' being painted on its surface, it was well known to the Germans, and this is a Luftwaffe bombing photograph taken by a reconnaissance aircraft on 23 November 1940. The airfield is marked 'A', though they have mistakenly included the area south of the River Penk, and Boulton Paul's factory is marked 'B'. Only one aircraft attacked Boulton Paul during the war, and its bombs hit the sewage beds at Barnhurst

In the fields to the north of Wolverhampton, near Featherstone, a huge ordnance factory was built early on in the war. This aerial view taken from 300ft, shows progress in April 1941. Part of the site is still operating, but much of it has been taken over by two large prisons.

A large shadow factory was built on the Stafford Road during the war, to house an expansion of H.M. Hobson's carburettor production, with the first machinists moving in from the Accuracy Works in June 1940. This aerial view shows the factory just after the war when an extra foundry block had been added to the right.

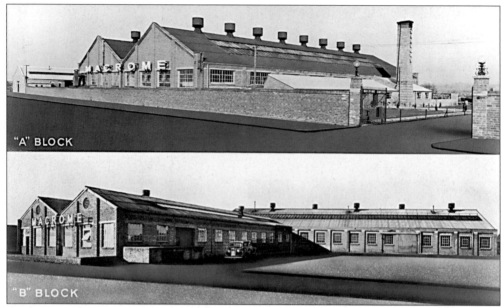

"A" BLOCK

"B" BLOCK

A pre-war Italian carpet factory in Aldersley was closed down in 1940 and the Italians were interned. The buildings then became a Ministry store. Macrome Ltd, who treated steel products with a special hardening process, were bombed out of their Hay Mills factory, and after a spell at Alcester, bought the Aldersley factory which was sited on both sides of what became Macrome Road. 'B' Block, shown in the lower photograph, was later sold to Laystall Engineering's Crankshaft Division, making Merlin crankshafts.

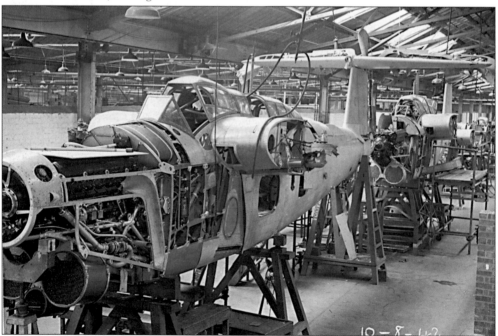

After Boulton Paul had built over 1,000 of their Defiants, the factory was turned over to production of the Fairey Barracuda naval dive-bomber, with the production line shown here in August 1942.

Courtauld's huge textile factory had moved to what remained of the Dunstall Hall site in Whitmore Reans in the 1920s. During the war much of the factory was turned over to war production, including the part which built Defiant wing centre sections. This is the ARP and fire service in 1940.

During the war the road under the Broad Street railway bridge, was lowered to allow double-decker buses to pass beneath. Up until that point, only single-decker trolley buses could operate on the Wednesfield route, like the one in the picture. Note the masked headlights, which only gave light through a narrow strip.

GRAMMAR SCHOOL, WOLVERHAMPTON.

Compton Road, with Wolverhampton Grammar School in the background as it looked during the war. The grammar school had moved to this site in 1890.

All over Wolverhampton, working men enlisted in the Home Guard, and this is the Zone H.Q. Company of the 23rd Battalion.

Goodyears was one of the largest factories in Wolverhampton, and very important to the war effort. There was a very large Goodyear Home Guard unit, of which this is just one platoon.

It is sometimes easy to forget that during the war a large chunk of ordinary life continued almost as normal, including ballet classes for little girls. Here Espinoza, founder of the British Ballet Organisation, gives instruction to pupils of the Vera Hildreth School in Waterloo Road, around 1943. He is holding the foot of Eileen Randle, and seated on the left is her sister Sheila.

On VE Day there were street parties all over the town. These ladies are attending a party in All Saints Road with their children. From left to right: John Parker, Janice Parker, Amy Parker, -?-, Nellie Emms, Grahame Hapley, Olive Hapley, Millie Swatman, Annette Swatman, -?-, -?-, -?-, Norma Bailey, Robin Bailey. Amy Parker was the little girl in the picture on p. 55, then Amy Emms. She was about the same age then, as the daughter that she is holding in this picture.

Six

1945-1960

The years after the end of the war were ones of continued struggle; the country was in a parlous financial position, rationing had to remain in place, and the cry was; 'Export or die!' Luckily the only viable industrial nation able to compete with Great Britain was the United States, so there was a ready market for British goods for a while, until the shattered industries of Europe had been rebuilt.

A new hope dawned with the Festival of Britain in 1951, seeming to signal an end to the austere years, and to herald a new age of Rock and Roll, Teddy Boys and the television. The town's motto 'Out of Darkness cometh Light' took on new meaning in those days.

Wolverhampton had not been badly hit by German bombing, but there was still much rebuilding work to be done, and the work of replacing slum housing, begun in the 1920s, would continue with new council estates ringing the town. The new era was mirrored by the fortunes of the town's football team, which often matched the mood of many Wulfrunians. The Wolves began their glory days with a win in the FA Cup Final in 1949, a marvellous era which was to end with another win in 1960.

A typical post war scene in Dudley Road looking towards Snow Hill. There are very few private cars on the roads, and both motor buses and trolley buses are serving the town. The Gaumont Palace, on the site of the old Agricultural Hall, was considered the premier cinema in the town, and as the age of Rock and Roll dawned in the 1950s, would be the venue for most pop concerts in Wolverhampton.

An aerial view looking across Neachells Lane and the LMS railway line towards Deans Road; the town centre can be seen in the distance. This whole area was a region of old mine workings, and would be turned into the huge Deans Road and Eastfield council estates in the 1950s. The cooling tower of Wolverhampton Corporation's Commercial Road power station is in the top left.

The Winter of 1946-1947 was well-known as being the worst in living memory, but this photograph was taken in 1949, looking up Broad Street just after it snowed in June !

Ten years after their failure against Portsmouth, the Wolves returned to Wembley and beat Leicester in the FA Cup Final. From left to right, back row: W. Crook, R. Pritchard, B. Williams, N. Shorthouse, T Springthorpe. Front Row: J. Hancocks, S. Smyth, Stan Cullis (manager), W. Wright, J. Pye, J. Dunn, J. Mullen. This victory was to herald a great era, both for the team and for the town.

Dudley Street in the 1950s, with the Dolcis shoe shop on the right, next to the Dudley Arms public house.

On the 23 July 1950, Sir Winston Churchill arrived in the town to address a large election rally at Molineux Stadium. He is shown here stepping out of his car at the Victoria Hotel, having driven in from Pendeford Airport.

For many children their first school outing after the war was the first they had ever experienced. These are children at St Luke's School, Blakenhall, about to climb aboard their Don Everall coaches for an outing to Trentham Gardens in 1948.

Class Four from Neachells Lane Infants School, Wednesfield, celebrate the Festival of Britain in 1951, with a musical production featuring tambourines, triangles and drums.

The St John's Ambulance and industrial nurses of the town hold their annual dinner in the early 1950s.

The post-war era was the age of the jet, and in 1950 at Pendeford Airport, Boulton Paul conducted taxiing trials with their experimental delta wing P111. The aircraft was equipped with the company's first power-assisted controls, which were soon to dominate its production.

Hardly a typical scene in a large industrial town, but in 1952 the Albrighton Hunt met at the Crown public house, on the Wergs Road. The Crown was at the time decorated with fine examples of topiary.

The Wolverhampton & South Staffordshire Technical College opened in Wulfruna Street in 1933, and although it has become a polytechnic and then a university, the building has changed very little since the 1950s.

The bottom of Victoria Street in the 1950s, with the Hippodrome still operating at the top. Don Everall's travel agency is on the right. Don Everall was famous in the town as a coach operator, but also ran a car agency, the airport, and a holiday airline.

The directors of H.M. Hobsons, striding confidentally across the car park in the 1950s. From left to right: Messrs Aiers, Searwright, Stokes, Hughes, and Clifford. With the decrease in the market for carburettors for use in piston-engined aircraft, the company had started making power control units. It was taken over by Lucas Aerospace, and is now TRW Aeronautical Systems Lucas Aerospace.

The employees of Don Everall (Aviation) Ltd at Wolverhampton Airport in the late 1950s. Some of their fleet of aircraft are ranged behind them, including a DC-3 airliner which normally operated holiday flights from Birmingham Airport, but was serviced at Wolverhampton.

The actor, Jack Hawkins (left), with Peter Clifford, who had inadvertently taxied the Bristol Freighter into the stream alongside Wolverhampton Airport. They were making the film 'The Man in the Sky', 1956, largely filmed at the airport and surrounding area.

The Royal School, floodlit, on the Penn Road; beginning as the town's orphanage on the same site in 1852, it became the Royal Orphanage in 1899.

In the 1950s, many of the Wolverhampton's young men became engineering apprentices when they left school, learning the trades which had made the town famous. These are the apprentices and their trainers at just one of the town's companies, Boulton Paul Aircraft in 1955. They are standing in front of a Balliol trainer, the last aircraft produced in the town.

Before the era of David and Victoria Beckham, Wolverhampton had its own glamorous couple, the famous footballer, Billy Wright, and the singer from an all girl group, Joy Beverley, of the Beverley Sisters. They are pictured here with the Mayor, Frank Mansell.

In 1960 Wolverhampton boasted two large breweries, Bank's in Chapel Ash and William Butler's Springfield Brewery. Here Ron Tranter is leaving the yard with a load of Springfield Bitter and other ales for customers across the West Midlands.

The victorious Wolves are taking the FA Cup on a tour of the town aboard a Don Everall coach, 1960. Huge crowds have gathered in Cheapside to see the team arrive at the town hall for a civic reception.

Seven

1960-1980

The sixties and seventies saw the biggest changes made to the town, more than any of the other decades in the twentieth century. Demolition continued on a large scale, especially to make way for the construction of the Mander and Wulfrun shopping centres and the ill-starred ring road. Rows of terraced houses were knocked down and large blocks constructed in their place. Concrete replaced bricks and mortar at every turn. Nowadays the loss of the Central and Queen's Arcades, the old indoor market and so many of the town's old buildings is looked upon as official vandalism on a huge scale. At the time it was seen as proud modernity in an era of a fashion and pop music revolution. The other big change to the town during these years was the multi-cultural revolution, as immigration brought diverse ethnic groups into the town

The Queen visited Wolverhampton in May 1962, and was introduced to local ethnic leaders outside the Civic Hall. The town was rapidly becoming an ethnically diverse community. During the visit she also presented a standard to the Queen's Own Royal Yeomanry at Molineux Stadium, and visited the Grammar School for its 450th Anniversary.

Though the sixties brought about many changes, one of town's traditions which remained unchanged was the May Day celebrations at All Saints School, something which had been taking place since 1912. This picture shows the May Pole dancing in 1962.

One of the features of the sixties was the demolition of many old buildings in the town, This is the 107 year-old retail market hall being knocked down in 1962. A new market has been built well away from the town centre.

A notice on the Congregational church in Queen Street says 'acquired', one of a number of churches in the town which were demolished in the 1960s and 1970s. The job centre now occupies the site – presumably with redundant vicars as early customers!

Two more buildings living on borrowed time, the wholesale market hall, and the Chequered Ball public house alongside. The retail market patch had become a car park, but the town's bureaucrats had their eyes on the whole site for the new Civic Centre.

The actress Noele Gordon, filming an episode of the soap opera Crossroads at Wolverhampton Airport in the 1960s. The extras in the background are all flying club members.

Air races and air displays were a feature of Wolverhampton Airport for many years, including the Royal Air Force Association's displays of the 1960s. The largest aircraft ever to land at the airport was this Blackburn Beverley in the 1967 Display. The airport closed in 1971 and became a housing estate.

The trolley buses were another casualty of the 1960s. This is the No. 13 to Bradmore, just passing through Prince's Square in 1963. The traffic lights, then in the centre of the square, were on the site of the first ever set of traffic lights in Europe.

The trolley buses were replaced by diesel buses, and this is a Guy Wulfrunian in 1968, waiting at the Tettenhall Wood stop in Queen Street, The Wulfrunian proved to be a disastrous design for Guy Motors, and ended their involvement in bus manufacture, which had been a feature of the town for half a century.

During the 1960s, working methods began to change considerably. Here, in 1960, electronic accounting machines are used to process the flow of orders for tools at Macrome Ltd, in Aldersley. Despite making some attempt to move with the times, this company was taken over by a rival in the 1970s and closed down, its buildings being taken over by Rothley Tube and Fern Plastics.

A company which did not move with the times, was the William Evans ironmongers in School Street. Shown in 1973 it remained open until the late 1990s, when, after closure, the first floor was found to be a time capsule of Victorian machinery.

The 1960s was the most famous decade for the revolution in pop music, and the Civic Hall was a popular venue for concerts and dances. Here revellers at the Boulton Paul apprentice's ball crowd the dance floor.

Ashland Street which is bisected by Merridale Street in 1973. This row of terraced houses was demolished soon afterwards, like many such rows which went in the 1960s and 1970s, usually to be replaced by flats and maisonettes. Ashland Street is symbolic of the end of this process, as in the middle portion of this street, half a dozen terraced houses still remain. At this point refurbishment, instead of demolition, became the fashion.

ENTRANCE, MOLINEUX PARK, WOLVES F.C., WOLVERHAMPTON   M 6348

The Molineux Hotel when it was still open in the 1960s, with the main entrance to the football ground's South Bank to the left. Since the construction of the ring road through the foreground of this picture, the building that was once Molineux House has become derelict, which is a source of shame to many Wulfrunians.

The fortunes of the town's football team plummeted in the 1960s, with relegation to the Second Division. The team captain, and one of the club's greatest players, Ron Flowers (centre) talks with Hugh McIlmoyle, as they walk out for the second half on a very muddy pitch. To the right is Peter Knowles, whose early retirement because of his religious beliefs is still lamented by Wolves' supporters.

It is often forgotten that the famous Chubb building, used by the lock-company until their move to the Wednesfield Road, was occupied for a long time by Baelz, who sold oil dispensing equipment. The building has now become offices with the Lighthouse Cinema alongside.

The slow and painful construction of Wolverhampton's ring road destroyed a swathe of buildings all around the town. This is a crowded Powlett Street in 1973, looking towards St John's church. All the buildings in the foreground were demolished for the St George's section of the ring road.

Bradburn and Wedge's car showroom at the corner of Salop Street, and the ring road in 1974. This was on the point of being demolished, as were all the buildings in the background at the bottom of Darlington Street. A building society office block now occupies the site.

The wholesale market being demolished in 1973; a new one has been built in Hickman Avenue.

An aerial view of part of the town centre in the sixties. The large building in the centre is the new C & A store on Dudley Street, with the roof of the Central Arcade a little further up the street. The Savoy Cinema, later the ABC, and now a night club, is in the foreground.

With the construction of the Mander Shopping Centre it was planned to rebuild the Central Arcade, and the start of this process can be seen here in 1973.

There was a disastrous fire in the Central Arcade just after the previous photograph was taken, the aftermath of which can be seen in this photograph, from the smoke-blackened facade. This resulted in the Arcade being demolished, to the regret of everyone in the town.

A picture of a rather leafier Chapel Ash, taken in July 1974. 'The Toy Shop' opposite the Clarendon Hotel was run by Tony and Wendy Hodgetts, who also ran the newsagents a little nearer to the town centre. This is now an arts supplies shop.

Eight

1980-2000

In the last two decades in the twentieth century, wholesale demolition began to be replaced with a new spirit of conservation. Buildings were refurbished wherever possible, and this lead to a curious process of creating pubs and nightclubs out of an increasingly varied range of locations, including banks, offices, courts and even a canal warehouse. Sadly, despite the council being anxious to conserve certain listed buildings, like The Royal Hospital, Molineux House, Low Level Station and the Springfield Brewery, it has not always been easy to find new uses, and the finance, to restore these buildings.

The recession of the early 1980s also put the final nail in the coffins of many of the great industrial names in the town, like Bayliss, Jones and Bayliss, ECC, Turner Engineering, Villiers, Guy Motors and John Thompsons. At the same time the creation of the University from the old Polytechnic, has made a huge difference to the nightlife of the town with the opening of countless night spots and theme pubs to serve the student population. Other areas of regeneration have seen the rebuilding of Molineux Stadium and the team to go with it, the reconstruction of Dunstall Park Racecourse and the rebuilding of the athletics stadium at Aldersley. Finally with the coming of the Metro, the tram returned to the streets of the town once more.

By 1980 Wolverhampton was an integrated multi-ethnic community typified by the class scene at St Andrew's Junior School in Whitmore Reans, with class teacher Wendy Landman explaining effective comprehension.

This is the Guy Motors drawing office and sales staff photographed outside the Guy Sports Club pavilion. Guy closed in the 1980s, the last of the town's many motor vehicle manufacturers to go, even though it was the only part of British Leyland, apart from Land Rover, to be making a profit.

For many years Wolverhampton had the distinction of two mainline railways stations side by side. Here a Castle Class locomotive leaves Low Level Station with an express for Birmingham in 1963. In 1981 Low Level closed, and has remained empty and increasingly derelict ever since. The Sun Street Bridge, seen on the photograph, has since been demolished.

The canal brought early prosperity to Wolverhampton, even before the railways, with Broad Street basin becoming a very busy 'port'. Taken in 1985, this photograph shows some of the old crowdedness of the canal with a gathering of narrow boats. The area continues to be redeveloped.

The Wolverhampton Association for Sport in Primary Schools (WASPS) runs a number of different sports in the town. This is the town's primary schools cross-country team for girls in 1990 at Tettenhall College, the venue for many cross-country races.

Not unlike a scene at several county cricket grounds, like Worcester. This is a local league match taking place on one of the many cricket pitches which used to exist on Dunstall Park Racecourse, with St Peter's and the floodlights of the Molineux in the background. The racecourse has now been completely redeveloped and this scene is no longer possible.

The VJ Day parade through Wolverhampton passes along Lichfield Street by the Art Gallery, in August 1945.

Part of the town's acknowledgement of its history, is the Civic Society's erection of blue plaques at significant locations. In 1997 Sunbeam cars, owned by members of the STD Register (Sunbeam Talbot Darraq), gathered at the site of one of Louis Coatalen's houses, Bromley House, when his daughter unveiled a plaque in his memory. This was the first time Sunbeam's chief engineer had been honoured by the town to which he had brought so much prestige.

A.E.'Ben' Gunn (right), chief test pilot of Boulton Paul Aircraft 1949-1965, opens the Boulton Paul Aircraft Heritage Project in October 1997 at the Dowty Aerospace factory. Alongside is Cyril Plimmer, chairman of the Boulton Paul Association.

Princess Diana visited the town in 1997 to open, amongst other things, the new Bilston Street police station. She drew large crowds, as she did wherever she went. In the top left hand corner is Doreen Seiboth, a councillor of many years standing and Acting Mayor at the time.

In the last year of the twentieth century, a tram pulls into the Metro terminus on Bilston Street. At the beginning of the century electric trams were just about to make an appearance on the town's streets; just before the end of the century they reappeared. At the beginning of the century the first cinema in the town was not far away from opening, at the end of the century the new cinema at Bentley Bridge had just opened. At each end of the century Wolves were in the First Division (though now with different status). The more things change, the more they remain the same!